THE
POWER
OF
SHARED
VISION

THE
POWER
OF
SHARED
VISION

How to Cultivate Staff
Commitment & Accountability

MICHAEL HENRY COHEN

CREATIVE
HEALTH CARE
MANAGEMENT

Softcover ISBN 13: 978-1-886624-92-4
ebook ISBN 13: 978-1-886624-93-1

Printed and bound in the United States of America

19 18 17 16 15   5 4 3 2 1

First Printing: March 2015

Cover and interior design by James Monroe Design, LLC.

For permission and ordering information, write to:

Creative Health Care Management, Inc.
5610 Rowland Road, Suite 100
Minneapolis, MN 55343-8905

chcm@chcm.com
or call: 800.728.7766 or 952.854.9015

www.chcm.com

DEDICATION

When I was diagnosed with Parkinson's disease in 2009, I was shaken to the core, fearing how it would affect my family and career. While conducting workshops, I became self-conscious of my involuntary tremors, believing they were distracting from my message. Against all rational thought, I was embarrassed by my symptoms, and I was seriously considering giving up my leadership and organizational development consulting practice.

After a significant amount of introspection, however, I decided to apply the self-management principles that I advocate in my workshops and books. Rather than feel sorry for myself, I chose to accept the disease as an aspect of life that is outside of my control and minimize its negative impact through physical therapy and medication. I chose to focus on things that *are* within my control, including my attitude, conduct, work ethic, and desire to serve. I chose to do the very best I can with the cards that I've been dealt. I will not let Parkinson's disease define who I am. That is all any of us can do.

This book is dedicated to persons living with neurological disorders and the people who love them.

CONTENTS

5

6

7

8

9

ACKNOWLEDGMENTS

First and foremost, I want to thank my wife, Jo Ellen Davey Cohen and my son, Jason Michael Cohen, for reading the initial drafts of this book and making constructive recommendations for improvement both in style and content. Without your encouragement, patience, and understanding, this book would not be possible.

Thank you to Ashish Bhatia, MD, FAAD, Assistant Professor of Clinical Dermatology, at Northwestern University School of Medicine, for doing me the honor of writing the Foreword to this book. Your compassion and interpersonal relationship skills are a model for other physicians to emulate.

Thank you to Creative Health Care Management (CHCM) for your mission and service-driven orientation. At every level within your organization, people conduct themselves in a professional and ethical manner. It is a pleasure to be associated with a business that consistently practices what it teaches.

In particular, I wish to thank Rebecca Smith, CHCM's Development Editor and Writing Coach, for your technical skills, creativity, and enthusiasm. You made the editing process truly enjoyable.

I'd also like to thank Chris Bjork, CHCM Resources Director for your friendship and support; Mary Koloroutis, MS, RN, Susan Cline, MBA, MSN, RN, NEA-BC, and Marty Lewis-Hunstiger, MS, RN, for participating in the peer review process; Jay Monroe for your original design concepts; Catherine Perrizo, MBA, for your meticulous proofreading of the book.

AUTHOR'S NOTE

ABOUT PRONOUNS AND GENDER NEUTRALITY

Throughout this book I have attempted to maintain gender neutrality by referring to employees, managers, and all others using a method of alternating masculine and feminine pronouns equally. I have chosen this method rather than overusing the sometimes cumbersome *he or she* or the grammatically not-yet-standard *they* when using a pronoun to refer to an individual in instances where the individual could be of either gender.

_____

*"Go into the world and do well.
But more importantly, go into the world
and do good."*

_____

MINOR MYERS, JR.
PRESIDENT, ILLINOIS WESLEYAN UNIVERSITY

FOREWORD

In medical school I learned a great deal about the art and science of taking care of patients. In contrast, there was very little formal education on leadership and management skills. This baffled me since I realized that these skills are essential for tending to the daily business of good patient care. These skills are critical today because medicine is now, more than ever before, a "team sport." Today's teams include multiple clinicians, clinical and administrative staff, and a broad range of ancillary service staff. Their combined efficiency and quality of service play a tremendous role in the success or failure of the organization as well as the health of our patients.

One way to keep these teams unified and help them deliver peak performance is by establishing a shared vision, and then consciously cultivating a deep commitment to that shared vision among your staff. When the shared vision is that of excellence in health care delivery, it has a positive effect upon the quality of care our patients receive, as well as upon the individuals on the health care team. For individuals, belief in a shared vision can bestow a sense of connection and loyalty to the team, increase motivation and effort, stimulate creative problem solving, and cultivate a desire to set a great example for others on the team. While a shared vision sets the direction for health care teams, a culture of commitment and accountability helps individuals stay on course to deliver results.

My first official position of management and leadership came when I was named the chief resident in my residency program. It was a dubious honor at best. The position calls for maintaining or exceeding the clinical workload of the other residents while managing your peers and performing administrative duties such as scheduling guest lecturers for grand rounds, as well as managing resident call schedules, resident vacation time, resident clinic schedules, and all educational activities for the residents and medical students. I was not fully prepared to lead my peers and serve as an intermediary between the attending physicians and the residents. I made my share of mistakes, but I learned from them. These hard-won lessons have served me well as an attending physician and in various leadership roles.

Soon after finishing residency and fellowship training, I was sharing what I had learned in my year as a chief resident with other former chief residents from programs around the country. We found that there were many common lessons that we all learned. We worked together to create the Chief Academy, a weekend workshop designed to provide leadership and management skills to the residents around the country who are chosen to be chief residents. We recruited a curriculum development team which included department chairs and program directors from the best residency programs around the country. Now, with nearly nine years of experience running and teaching at the Chief Academy, I still gain knowledge and insight at this program. These management skills and lessons are relevant to all aspects of health care, especially clinical practice. Many former graduates of Chief Academy return to volunteer as faculty and share their experiences and lessons.

One of the most rewarding parts of my job, second only to helping my patients, is developing people. Establishing a culture of commitment and accountability, as described by Mike Cohen, helps individuals on our teams grow personally and professionally. As a manager, it is a magnificent feeling to watch someone develop in this way. Contributing to a person's professional and personal growth gives me a great sense of pride and accomplishment because I have helped them develop skills that will help in all walks of life, whether their path takes them up the ladder in our organization or elsewhere.

Leadership takes a bit of selflessness. It also requires wanting to establish a standard that is taught by example. Here are some of the common phrases that I find myself, and now our designated and undesignated leaders on both the administrative and clinical sides of the practice, repeating over and over:

1. If you are not getting better, you are getting worse. There is no status quo. Constantly work to improve your skills.

2. Lead by example.

3. Always act professionally and provide an excellent patient experience.

4. Care for our patients and their families as you would want others to care for your own. If you do so, you will nearly always make good decisions.

5. If you enjoy what you do every day, work is not work.

While this concise handbook is broad enough in its reach to be of great value to any manager in any field, I can confirm for anyone not in the know that it provides all of the essentials of management and leadership in health care. By using Michael Cohen's staff engagement and accountability principles, anyone in a leadership role can help people to do their best, feel a sense of accomplishment, and contribute to an organization's shared vision for success. I also agree with Mike Cohen's assertion that for a work team to be successful, everyone must take personal responsibility for their conduct and the effect it has on others. Personal accountability leads to a more professional and satisfying work environment for everyone.

Everyone in a leadership role in a practice, hospital, or other health care setting should read *The Power of Shared Vision* and then reread it periodically. It should be made available to any employee who demonstrates even an inkling of leadership potential. It should be required reading for every physician. At the very least it makes sense that when providing direction to enhance high quality patient care, you should know how to increase the chances that your directives are carried out in the way they were intended.

Looking at my experiences from my early days as a hospital volunteer in high school to being a department chairman in a 450+ physician multispecialty group, I realize that health care is a unique field. Here, excellence in management *and* patient care need to co-exist to truly serve our customers. A deficiency in either can have a wide range of consequences, from the loss of a dissatisfied patient to the loss of a life. A consistent observation in my 25 years in health care is that leadership can come from all ranks in the health care delivery system, and many times the people who are positioned to provide leadership are the least equipped to do so. Often, it is either because they don't have experience in managing people or they have not had any formal training in leadership.

If you are in a position of leadership and find yourself facing some management challenges, there are essentially three ways to learn the skills you'll need to be a good leader:

1. Trial and error (a long, costly, and often painful pathway to learning)

2. By emulation or example (if you are fortunate enough to have a good example)

3. Through didactic training (not necessarily an MBA, but even a short course or a

well-chosen leadership book such as the one you're currently holding)

In this book, Michael Cohen has crystalized the essentials of leadership and management needed to do well and *to do good* in the health care space or any other venue in which group commitment to a shared vision is essential to success. By harnessing the power of shared vision, anyone in health care can help lead people to do their best and contribute to an organization while improving their own skills and feeling a sense of accomplishment. It is my desire that leaders at all levels in health care will see the value in learning the basics of leadership and management, and will take steps to become good leaders by reading, internalizing, reflecting upon, and discussing the fundamental principles in this valuable book.

Ashish C. Bhatia, MD, FAAD

Associate Professor of Clinical Dermatology, Northwestern University—Feinberg School of Medicine
Chairman—Department of Dermatology, DuPage Medical Group Medical Director for Dermatologic Research - Department of Clinical Research, DuPage Medical Group
Director of Dermatologic, Laser & Cosmetic Surgery, The Dermatology Institute—Naperville, DuPage Medical Group

INTRODUCTION

A shared vision is an aspirational description of what a work group can accomplish when people are committed to achieving a common goal. A shared vision creates a sense of purpose and direction. It provides coherence to the diverse activities that occur within a work unit and establishes a group identity. The very process of developing a shared vision shifts the focus from the manager's goals to "our" goals (Senge, 1990, pp. 192-211).[1]

The concept of a shared vision is predicated on the belief that when employees participate in the decision-making process on issues that directly impact their job, they embrace the decision as their own and feel a positive emotional connection with their manager, job, and organization.

A shared vision has the power to transcend individual self-interests, personality, and work style differences. When commitment to the shared vision is strong, people simply find ways to effectively communicate

---

1. Senge, P. (1990). *The fifth discipline: The art and practice of the learning organization*. New York, NY: Doubleday/Currency.

and cooperate with one another in order to achieve desired results. When employees help establish boundaries by agreeing to reasonable standards of conduct, they take responsibility and accept the consequences of their actions. This in turn creates a safe and secure work environment that is conducive to achievement.

The alternative to establishing a culture of employee engagement and accountability is to accept mediocre performance, a litany of excuses, and a plethora of unhappy people who feel immune from the consequences of their actions. Without a strong belief system and an adherence to bedrock principles that are the foundation of all effective work teams, staff unity splits into disparate parts; different factions form as personal agendas get served and pettiness thrives.

The Power of Shared Vision addresses how to:

- Develop goals that unite people around a common cause and secure employee ownership of changes that improve the quality of their work.

- Create a retribution-free communication environment where people can tell the manager what she needs to hear without fear of retribution. In turn, the manager will be able to help her team distinguish problems that can be solved from those work realities that are outside of her control.

- Understand the reasons why some employees cannot or will not meet job-related expectations and what the manager can do to close the performance gap.

The Power of Shared Vision explains why the manager must establish personal credibility before he attempts to make significant changes that impact how employees perform their jobs. It discusses how to engage employees as internal consultants to develop performance standards and secure their commitment for achieving desired outcomes. It explores the appropriate use of organizational politics to access the permissions and resources needed to accomplish the shared vision of your department or work area.

This book also addresses how to coach employees who are technically competent but have a negative attitude. It explains how to set specific and behaviorally concise goals that support professional growth. It also outlines the documentation requirements necessary to ensure employees due process and to protect you from a claim of unfair management practices.

The Power of Shared Vision is exceedingly practical and grounded in reality. Whether you are a new or seasoned manager, you will find the book to be a valuable resource for achieving outstanding results.

*The sole advantage of power
is that you can do more good.*

BALTASAR GRACIÁN Y MORALES

THE ESSENCE OF
LEADERSHIP

Leadership does not require a charismatic personality or the ability to deliver a motivational speech. Words intended to inspire are vacuous if not followed up with concrete action, and charisma in the wrong hands can be a very dangerous thing.

Leadership does not come from position, title, credentials, or degrees. Leaders win support and influence people based on the strength of their character. Their primary source of power is personal credibility. They have earned people's trust and are respected for their knowledge, integrity, and good will.

Leadership is not the same as knowing how to effectively delegate tasks, monitor and evaluate performance, or mete out consequences for inappropriate conduct. Management techniques not grounded in values are simply gimmicks.

A leader's actions are underpinned by a vision of what can be accomplished when people rally around a common goal that transcends individual self-interest. Ultimately, a leader's legacy is determined by measurable outcomes achieved through ethical conduct, respectful language, and effective decisions.

As a consultant in organizational development, I have been blessed with the opportunity to work with a variety of outstanding leaders. While all of them have their own unique styles that contribute to their success, they all share five common characteristics:

- They lead by example.

- They have no pretenses or hidden agendas.

- They are passionate about what they do, and their enthusiasm is contagious.

- They have the courage to set and maintain high performance standards. They are demanding of themselves and others. Employees respect their

leader's tenacity and take pride in seeing positive
results.

- They are sensitive to the psychosocial needs of
  employees. Their primary focus, however, is on
  creating high quality products or services. They
  believe that happiness on the job is largely a
  byproduct of success.

The Quality of Employees Affects a Leader's Success

Successful leaders are acutely aware that their
effectiveness is contingent on attracting and retaining
employees whom they can depend on and trust. They
are continuously scanning their environment in search
of people who display confidence and competence,
genuinely enjoy their jobs, and demonstrate self-moti-
vation fueled by pride and the desire to contribute.

These employees don't view themselves as captive,
victimized, or powerless regardless of their situation.
The idea that someone is entitled to a job is foreign to
them. They don't allow another person's negative attitude to control their emotions. Because their focus is on
doing their job, they don't have the time or inclination

to complain or gossip. They choose their battles carefully and ask for what they want in a direct, honest, and constructive manner. They listen to the other person's perspective and are open to change.

These personality traits are indicators of high emotional intelligence. They are crucial to each person's ability to get cooperation from others, exercise self-control under difficult circumstances, and take responsibility for his own actions. Because these traits are highly valued and in demand, people who possess them can be selective about where they are going to work and for whom. They typically choose to work for managers who are goal-focused and results-driven and who maintain high performance standards for everyone. They enjoy being members of a well-functioning team.

If you pair an employee with high emotional intelligence with a dogmatic and disrespectful manager, the employee is likely to make a good-faith attempt to develop a constructive relationship. If the conflict between them can't be resolved, the employee will leave the toxic work environment when the time and conditions are to her advantage. This is the marketplace in action; talented and emotionally intelligent people ultimately vote with their feet.

A Leader Knows Her Limitations

Many of the personality traits that contribute to an employee's success or failure are outside of a manager's control. For example, you can't motivate a person to care. There are simply some people who shouldn't be working within the service industry. Employees who exhibit "TDC" (thinly disguised contempt) toward customers would be better off working in a lighthouse or another place where human interaction is not required.

You can create scripts that prescribe words employees should use so that customers feel respected and valued. Properly applied, scripts can lock in consistency on how employees relate to customers. But ultimately it's not what you say; it's how you say it that matters. Two employees can say the same words and come across quite differently based on their attitude and level of sincerity. Tone of voice and body language make all the difference. If there is not a genuine regard for the customer, words are empty.

You can't make someone play nice with others. The technology of being civil is not very complex. Respect and courtesy should be taught at home and expected in the classroom. If a person did not acquire social skills as a child, it may be too late for him to change significantly by the time he enters the work-place. It may take a significant emotional event in his life to make him understand the need for developing his interpersonal relationship skills.

You can strive to create a retribution-free com-munication environment in which people can speak their minds without fear of retaliation. However, your efforts to improve the manager-employee relationship can still be sabotaged by a negative opinion leader who is generally stirring the pot of discontent, com-plaining about you to higher ups, and hoping you will quit in despair or get fired.

You can create policies, procedures, and proto-cols that describe how a job is to be performed, but you can't teach common sense. No amount of rules will compensate for poor judgment. Likewise, you can mandate that employees demonstrate ethical conduct within the workplace, but your mandate will have minimal impact on a person who lacks integrity or character.

You can conduct a workshop on effective assertive-ness and conflict-management techniques, but your presentation will have little effect on those employees who fear confrontation and/or avoid conflict at all costs. Assertiveness is more about courage than skill.

You can preach the importance of punctuality, but you have no control over an employee who is frequently tardy to work. It's not your job to provide an early morning wake-up call. You can enhance an employee's technical skills through training and development if the person has the willingness and capacity to learn. You don't, however, have the time or ability to significantly change an employee's core personality.

Be Selective in Your Hiring Practices

Your department will never realize its full potential to achieve your shared vision until you have the right employees in the right positions. It is critical, therefore, that you select and retain only those people who have built into their character the value of hard work, the desire to serve, and the will to achieve. Even if you are short-staffed and desperate for a warm body, hold out until you find the right person. Competent employees would prefer to work short-handed for a sustained period of time than have to deal with a dysfunctional co-worker every day.

Selecting and holding on to the best available people is not optional; it's a precondition for success. In the face of organizational restructuring, mergers, and reductions in staff, you need employees who are flexible, adaptable, and have a high tolerance for ambiguity. When searching for a solution to a complex or long-standing problem, you need people who are patient, determined, and open to new ideas.

In the throes of conflict, you need employees who know how to tell others what they want in a plain-spoken, forthright, calm manner. They have successfully faced the challenge of learning how to be treated well. Because you are often pulled away from the department to attend meetings, you need self-managed people who are committed enough to do the right thing when no one is looking.

Ultimately, the employees you hire, promote, and retain on your team are a reflection on you and the values you hold.

Discussion Questions

Identify a leader (manager, teacher, coach, relative, etc.) who served as a role model for you, believed in your capacity for personal or professional growth, and made a significant difference in your life. Describe the person's specific leadership qualities.

It is said that a manager can't motivate someone to care. Do you agree? What can a manager do to facilitate a person's drive to succeed?

Example is not the main thing in influencing others; it's the only thing.

ALBERT SCHWEITZER

LEADERSHIP IS A
BALANCING ACT

Successful leaders are able to inspire people to hold themselves accountable for high-quality performance while maintaining a positive work environment conducive to employee engagement and satisfaction. They understand that accomplishing goals and establishing positive employee relationships are not mutually exclusive objectives. Balance is the key to their success.

If you are primarily concerned with being liked or are overly focused on making people happy, you may unintentionally lower performance standards in order to avoid conflict and maintain harmony. As a result:

- People underachieve and don't grow professionally.

- Quality of work diminishes.

- People come to believe that you are responsible for their engagement and satisfaction, and feel entitled to their jobs.

- You ultimately lose the respect of both your employees and your boss for tolerating mediocrity.

On the other hand, if you are overly focused on meeting deadlines and accomplishing goals, it may appear that you don't care about how people feel or that you view them only as useful tools for getting things done. In this case, you find yourself adopting a command and control leadership style, using fear and intimidation as your primary "motivational" strategies. You'll make decisions without employee input, dictate how employees will perform tasks, and punish employees who dare to question your decisions. In this kind of environment:

- Employees will avoid you as much as possible. They will cringe whenever you approach them, expecting to be lambasted for something they did wrong.

- People will become tentative in their actions, fearing that a mistake will provoke your wrath.

- People will tell you what you want to hear. They know by experience that you punish the bearers of bad news and have a low tolerance for diversity of opinions.

- People will turn to the Human Resources Department or an outside agency to help protect them from your capricious and arbitrary actions.

- The very best employees will look for another job and for a manager who respects and acknowledges people for their contributions.

Adopting an autocratic management style can be very seductive because it is, in theory, so uncomplicated. You simply tell people what to do and punish them for non-compliance. This style lends itself to fast decision-making because you don't have to listen to every point of view or explain your actions.

In the long run, however, you get better results when people embrace department goals as their own. Making demands and threats may work in the short term, but ultimately your success is contingent upon the actions of people who are intrinsically motivated to produce the highest quality product or service possible.

The Leader as Change Agent

The quality of performance within your department either improves or declines. It never stays the same. While it is critical that you recognize individual and team achievements, you should never be completely satisfied with the status quo. By definition, effective leaders are facilitators of positive change.

The first step to becoming an effective change agent is establishing your personal credibility. People have to believe in you, your values, and your vision for the department before they will become committed to your agenda. When it becomes "our agenda" true success is achieved. Shared ownership becomes possible because employees feel heard, seen, and valued. This includes demonstrating that you understand the history and culture of the group before you introduce change that will significantly impact their work.

Credibility is a subjective leadership quality. It is based on employees' perceptions of your intentions and the meaning they attach to your behavior. In short, credibility is in the eyes of the beholder. To establish credibility, employees must believe that you possess knowledge, character, good will, and decency.

Knowledge

You speak with authority. Your judgment is sound. You have the mental capacity and the job-related experience to lead. You are competent. You also ask and listen. You value your team as a source of expertise and knowledge.

Character

You are a person of integrity, and you consistently demonstrate that you can be trusted. You keep your promises and honor your commitments. You harbor no hidden agenda. You model the attitude and behaviors expected of others.

Good Will

You are genuinely supportive of employees. You are their most ardent advocate and spokesperson. You are motivated to set people up for success and help them look good in the eyes of others. You enjoy recognizing individuals and teams for achievement and promoting their professional development. You do not take public credit for your employees' work, but rather honor their contributions consistently and publicly.

Decency

You have an even temperament. During stressful situations, you remain calm and collected, as evidenced by your appropriate choice of language and tone of voice. You are unconditionally respectful toward people. Employees are comfortable and well disposed toward you.

10 Ways to Earn Professional Credibility

1. Lead by example. Model the attitude and behaviors expected of employees.

2. Communicate your vision and the values and principles that underpin your actions.

3. Honor your commitments.

4. Strive to be open and transparent with employees. Tell them what they need to hear. Be straight with them.

5. Demonstrate your expertise. You don't have to be the most technically competent person in your department to be credible, but employees expect you to have a level of knowledge and skill before they will follow your lead.

6. Set and maintain high performance standards, and help people understand how to hold themselves accountable for outstanding outcomes. Follow through to assure that accountability is achieved. Remember that the appearance of favoritism will diminish your credibility.

7. Be accessible and approachable.

8. Roll up your sleeves and offer a helping hand when the need exists.

9. Treat people with unconditional respect, especially during stressful or conflict-laden situations. This is when your character is put to the test.

10. Achieve measurable results over a sustained period of time through ethical conduct and sound judgment.

How Your Own Behavior Can Undermine Your Credibility

Some managers have been known to exhibit behaviors that contribute to a hostile work environment. They use their positional power to threaten and intimidate employees. They are condescending and demeaning. They lose control in stressful or conflict-laden situations. They yell, interrupt, swear, or call people derogatory names.

Some managers display passive-aggressive behaviors toward employees they personally don't like in order to induce a "voluntary resignation." They:

- Establish unreasonable deadlines and/or create a huge workload that is impossible to complete.

- Delegate tasks that are beyond the employee's skills or training.

- Assign meaningless activities that create a feeling of uselessness.

- Deliberately withhold resources necessary to accomplish a task.

- Micro-manage the employee, hovering over him, watching every move he makes.

- Withhold recognition for doing a good job while praising others.

- Criticize the employee in front of peers and/or customers.

- Become inaccessible, unapproachable, or unresponsive to the employee's questions or requests.

- Show contempt or disdain for the person by using the silent treatment or exhibiting impolite conduct.

Employees who observe this malicious behavior toward one of their colleagues wonder who will be next to experience the manager's wrath. Trust is eroded and their relationship with the manager becomes guarded. The working environment becomes toxic. There is no doubt that performance suffers.

Holding Yourself Accountable

- Model the attitude and behaviors expected of others. Lead by example.

- Don't waste time focusing on things outside your control. Instead of complaining about how others

are preventing you from accomplishing your goals,
examine what you are doing that is getting in the way
of progress.

- Take ownership of your mistakes. Don't cover them
  up, make excuses, or blame someone else.

- Commit 100% to what you are doing. If your
  commitment begins to wane, strive to rekindle it.
  Don't easily succumb to obstacles that come your
  way. Explore, search, and question: "What else can I
  do to achieve my objective?"

- Honor your commitments.

- Express appreciation when people provide you with
  feedback that you may not want, but need to hear.

- Don't feel that you are captive, victimized, or
  powerless when faced with work frustrations. Identify
  all of your available choices and take responsibility
  for the outcome of your decisions.

- Enjoy and celebrate positive outcomes.

The Leader as Power Broker and Politician

An important step in becoming an effective change agent is learning how to use your positional power and political acumen to accomplish your objectives. Power and politics are not dirty words. Having power means that you have the capacity to produce a desired outcome. Being politically savvy means that you have identified those people who can help or hinder the accomplishment of your goals and have secured from them the support and resources necessary for success.

In order to ensure that you are on solid footing politically, start by ensuring that your own manager is on board with your objectives and methods of implementation. Next, review the organizational chart to determine reporting relationships. Although the organizational chart may not represent how things really happen, it does reveal official levels of authority. Finally, identify informal opinion leaders within your own department. These are employees who don't have official positional power, but shape and influence co-workers' attitudes.

The purpose of the above exercise is to determine up front who are your allies, skeptics, and potential opponents of the change you are proposing. Once identified, you want to:

- Energize your allies by placing them in positions of influence.

- Invite the skeptics into the process by legitimizing their doubts and using them as a sounding board to test out ideas. Ask them to help you create a change that adequately addresses their concerns.

- Think through a strategy to convert opponents of the change to your side. If this is not possible, find a way to minimize the negative impact their opposition has on others within the department.

- Deal forthrightly with those people who are actively undermining the change by constantly complaining without offering alternative suggestions.

Accomplishing your goals is contingent on understanding and accepting the fact that politics is an inherent part of organizational life. Rather than becoming consumed with indignation about the "office politics" in your organization, use politics to your advantage. It is not a compromise of your integrity or character to be an effective advocate for a worthy goal, and there is no point to acquiring power if you're not going to use it to create positive change.

Myths about the Role of Politics in Organizational Life

The following myths were distilled from an exercise I do in my professional workshops. Through countless discussions with managers in the field, I have identified these commonly held myths and have debunked them for you here.

MYTH: A new manager promoted from within her work unit can remain best of friends with some of her former peers.

The unfortunate reality is that it is a real challenge to be promoted within your own work unit. Your new role gives you authority over your former peers, some of whom may be your best friends. You now are called upon to make out assignments, evaluate performance, and, if necessary, administer corrective action. Some employees may advance the theory that you have changed or that the newly acquired power has gone to your head. The fact is, you're the same person; it's the relationship that has changed.

You may claim that you have in the past or are currently supervising your best friend without any difficulty. There is no reason to doubt your sincerity. However, even an unwarranted suspicion of favoritism can diminish a manager's credibility. Continue your close personal relationships with direct reports at your own risk.

MYTH: Self-motivated and results-driven people don't need the same amount of positive feedback or recognition as employees who are not as self-directed.

Not true. All people, including your top performers, need recognition for doing a good job, provided the feedback is perceived to be sincere and warranted. Those behaviors that are reinforced tend to get repeated. Likewise, you run the risk of extinguishing good behavior by taking it for granted.

Your top performers are very employable people. They can take their skills with them wherever they work. Give them a reason to stay. Recognizing them for achievement is a good place to start.

MYTH: Employees' lack of knowledge or technical skills is the number one cause of customer complaints.

The truth is that the most frequent customer complaints are about a bad attitude, perceived indifference, or lack of respect. You can make a mistake technically, and if you catch it quickly the customer will probably not know the difference, and may even appreciate your efforts to get the problem corrected. However, people know when they're treated with impatience or contempt.

MYTH: A manager is at least 50% responsible for an employee's job satisfaction and motivation.

While one of a manager's responsibilities is to create a positive environment that facilitates employee job satisfaction, each person is 100% responsible for his own motivation and attitude. You may be a competent and caring person, engaged in state-of-the-art leadership practices, and there still may be a handful of employees who continuously complain. Nothing you do will ever satisfy them.

It is essential to remember, however, that a self-motivated employee will do a good job even if she reports to an incompetent manager. If she finds it impossible to maintain a positive attitude because of bad management practices, she will find another job that is conducive to her job success and satisfaction. People have choices about where they're going to work and for whom.

MYTH: During social occasions such as coffee breaks, lunch engagements, staff parties, and dinners, it's fine to be candid about some of the negative experiences or dissatisfactions you're having at work.

Even in these situations, you're being sized up by your employees. Every social interaction you have with co-workers creates an impression which either adds to or diminishes your credibility. Although these social gatherings are voluntary and take place on unpaid time, what you say and do has consequences.

You also don't want to become the life of the party. If you're wearing a lampshade on your head before the night is over, you might not be respected in the morning. If, on the other hand, you really don't enjoy company parties, come late or leave early, but at least make an appearance if at all possible. If you never attend these gatherings, you may convey the message that you're not a part of the team.

MYTH: Being open and honest about your personal feelings toward your manager and co-workers is generally a good policy.

Nope. Your manager and co-workers don't need to know how you feel about them. It would be a dangerous workplace if people always shared their innermost thoughts about one another. The truth does not always set you free, and brutal honesty is not necessarily a virtue.

Liking someone is not a pre-condition for maintaining a healthy, productive professional relationship. The mission of your organization and the goals of your department transcend your personality conflicts or differences in communication style. Regardless of personal feelings, your role is to set your manager and co-workers up for success and help them look good in the eyes of the customer.

I am not recommending that you be dishonest in your relationships. I am suggesting, however, that discretion is the better part of valor.

Sometimes it's helpful to give the impression that things are better than they actually are.

MYTH: The closer you get to an employee and the more involved you become in his personal problems and aspirations, the more likely you are to get cooperation from him.

It's a nice thought, but it puts you in a problematic position. Don't get so close to an employee that you're expected to accept his performance deficiencies. Know enough about an employee's personal problems to determine if an accommodation is appropriate or if the services of an Employee Assistance Program are indicated. Be supportive of an employee's career goals and aspirations, but remain objective enough to make decisions that are in the best interests of the organization.

MYTH: As a manger, you must be absolutely fair and consistent with people in order to win credibility and be effective in your job.

When you give it some thought, you'll see that the terms "absolute" and "fair" are inherently contradictory. Absolute suggests that you are free from imperfection and limitations or that your decisions and actions are not to be questioned. Fairness, on the other hand, is a relative term. It suggests that your decisions and actions are subject to interpretation and evaluation.

Most people say they want their manager to be "absolutely consistent and fair" in decisions that impact their work, until a situation arises in which they feel an accommodation should be made on their behalf. You are being paid to make judgment calls that may be difficult to objectify. You can't wait to make a decision until you secure everyone's agreement. Leadership sometimes requires the courage to take a stand on positions that are unpopular and that may seem unfair to some.

MYTH: As long as you do what's right for your customers and employees, it shouldn't matter whether or not you have a positive relationship with your manager or if she is satisfied with your work.

For better or worse, your manager has control of the permissions and resources you need to accomplish your goals. She can choose to be your best ally or a thorn in your side. A good relationship with your manger makes it more likely that she will support you when you make an unpopular decision or when a group of employees challenges your authority. I am not advocating that you become a "yes person" or engage in unethical practices to please your manger. However, you have to deal with the world as it is, not as you wish it would be. You enhance your job security when your manager is satisfied with your work and you have established a relationship based on openness and trust.

This myth has one big caveat: While satisfying your manager is undeniably important, your *first* concern should be doing what's in the best interests of your employees and the customers they serve, not in pleasing your boss. Strive to excel because you take pride in accomplishment and enjoy seeing the positive results of your efforts.

MYTH: Failing to address an employee's negative attitude or technical incompetence has little effect on department morale or the reputation of the manager.

If only it were so. Conscientious people resent a manager who does not hold everyone accountable for meeting high performance standards. After all, *they* come to work as their schedule requires, work hard, and follow the rules. Why should other people get a pass? Employees don't always know if corrective action is being administered to others, but if the problematic behavior is long-standing, they assume that no action is being taken. This dampens their enthusiasm and contributes to cynicism.

Discussion Questions

Effective managers balance accomplishing goals with demonstrating sensitivity to peoples' needs and expectations. What are the consequences if a manager can't find this delicate balance?

Why is it desirable to establish your credibility and understand the history and culture of your department before making any significant changes?

Leadership is influence.

JOHN C. MAXWELL

3

PARTNERING WITH EMPLOYEES TO CREATE CHANGE

As a change agent, the burden is on you to convince your team that the present system is not working as well as it should and that the proposed change will make their job easier and more satisfying and/or improve the customer experience. People get comfortably routinized in how they manage their daily activities. Therefore, you must be prepared for ambivalence if not active resistance to goal accomplishment.

Employee skepticism should be considered a natural part of the change process. You deal with it by listening and empathizing with peoples' perceptions. Right or wrong, these perceptions are real, and have to be addressed. Anticipate and plan for the following objections:

- "There is no real need to change. What we are doing now is fine."

- "This change won't work."

- "Where has it been tried before?"

- "We don't have the time to do this."

- "We tried something just like this before, and it didn't work."

- "We are already overloaded."

- "We don't have the knowledge or skills to make this happen."

- "We may have a better idea."

The worst response to this kind of resistance is to become personally defensive or to punish people who express doubt about the change. The highest form of loyalty a person can demonstrate is telling you in a respectful manner what you need to hear, not necessarily what you want to hear.

To address their concerns, meet with your team to discuss all the key elements of the change process. Constant communication is critical to ensuring that they understand:

- Why the status quo is no longer acceptable.

- How the goal satisfies the need for improvement.

- What goal accomplishment will look like in verifiable terms.

- How the goal will be accomplished (applicable policies, procedures, and protocols to be respected).

- Specifics about where each person's job begins, ends, or overlaps with other members of the team.

- What resources (materials, supplies, equipment, training, coaching) exist to facilitate employee success.

- Potential barriers to accomplishment.

- How the results will be monitored and evaluated.

- What's in it for them.

If you involve people in the decision-making process on issues that directly impact their work, they are more likely to take ownership of the decision and implement it effectively. Therefore, utilize people as internal consultants by inviting them to critique decisions you are considering making, before you implement them. In cultures in which employees have a high level of expertise and ownership of the work, encourage them to take the lead in designing the work.

Characteristics of People Who Manage Change Effectively

Some people experience change as a threat. They hold on tenaciously to the status quo and resist anything new, regardless of its merits. If the change is inevitable, however, you need to help these people let go of the past and look for ways to make the change work.

Listed below are the characteristics of people who accept and adjust to change:

- They are confident of their ability to handle whatever the future brings. Instead of becoming consumed with worry and doubt, they anticipate, plan, and prepare. They choose to excel in times of change.

- They adapt well to any situation and approach change in a creative and resourceful manner. They are comfortable with ambiguity and uncertainty.

- They don't rush to judgment or take premature stands on issues. They are open-minded and have a high tolerance for diverse points of view.

- They place the change in proper context. They see the big picture.

- They enjoy learning. They view change as a welcome challenge and an opportunity for professional growth.

- They work for the success of the change regardless of their personal misgivings.

Securing Employee Commitment

Commitment is the act of binding oneself, intellectually and psychologically, to a course of action. It implies allegiance to a goal and determination to deliver on agreed-upon results.

The depth of employee commitment is a critical factor in any change management process. Therefore, once the nature, function, and scope of the change are understood, further align the team by asking for a commitment from each employee that signifies:

- I understand and embrace the change.

- I understand my specific role and responsibilities in helping to implement the change.

- I know what I don't know and am willing to acquire the necessary skills to meet performance expectations.

- Throughout the change process, I accept complete responsibility for my conduct and the impact it has on others.

Securing commitment should be an integral part of any goal setting process. Consider soliciting a commitment in any of these contexts:

- During departmental new employee orientation when job responsibilities are discussed.

- Following an employee's performance appraisal when establishing goals for the coming evaluation period.

- During a coaching session or when administering a corrective action to assess the person's understanding of the need for behavioral change.

- Within the context of team building when discussing the interdependency that exists (between work units, shifts, and job classifications), and the need to meet each other's expectations.

An Employee Agreement Template for Goal Accomplishment

Employee Performance Agreement for: _____

Position: _____

Manager: _____

Use this form to document the specific goal(s) you are committing to achieving. Use a separate form for each goal. If necessary, use additional pages to ensure a thorough response to each item.

Goal to Be Met: _____

Indicators of Success: Make sure that results to be achieved are stated in measurable (quantifiable) or observable (narrative) terms.

Potential Obstacles to Meeting Goal: Explain how you will overcome, adjust to, or minimize the negative impact of obstacles in order to meet performance expectations.

Things You Need from Your Manager to Facilitate Success: I affirm that the goal(s) named above are reasonable and attainable, and I hold myself accountable for attaining the agreed-upon results.

Signature of Employee: _____ Date _____

Signature of Manager: _____ Date _____

Discussion Questions

Why is it important to respect and acknowledge employee ambivalence and constructive resistance to proposed change?

Do you agree that the burden is on the manager to demonstrate that the status quo is no longer acceptable and that the proposed change will make employees' jobs easier, more effective, and more satisfying or improve quality and/or the customer experience? Please explain.

*If you don't know where you're going,
you'll end up someplace else.*

YOGI BERA

4

DEVELOPING GOALS THAT COUNT

Goals provide people with something of value to strive for, and unite them behind a common purpose. Goals provide direction and structure. Without professional goals, we are aimless and stagnant.

Goals can be individual or team-based, short-term or long-term, and can cover a wide variety of objectives. There are four types of goals from which to choose, depending on individual or team needs:

- Performance improvement goals to address identified deficiencies.

- Professional development goals to increase employees' knowledge base or skill set.

- Innovative goals to encourage creative thinking, experimentation, and state-of-the-art practices.

- Operational improvement goals to ensure that policies, procedures, and protocols are efficient and user-friendly for both employees and customers.

Goals should be recorded, reviewed regularly, shared widely, and modified as needed. They should also be integrated into the performance appraisal process and, if appropriate, weighted to signify their importance relative to other performance expectations.

The most effective goals challenge people to work outside their comfort zones in order to reach their full potential. As daunting as a goal may be, people will meet the challenge as long as they understand the benefits of achieving the goal, are aware of what they don't know and have the desire to learn, have the physical and mental capacity to achieve the goal, and have a leader who believes in them and who provides the necessary resources to succeed.

Establish Your Priorities

Some goals are more important than others. If you have an abundance of priorities, all of them important, you have no priorities. You have no focus. One definition of leadership is "the effective management of attention."

There's not enough time or resources for an organization or department to be great at everything. There are a few key results areas, however, where outstanding performance is critical. Your department stands for excellence in these areas and will stake its reputation on them.

Unlike mission, vision, and values statements, what you stand for should be expressed in short, easy-to-remember terms. For example, Walt Disney created an entertainment dynasty by standing for excellence in three key results areas:

- Cutting-edge visual effects

- Wholesome, family-oriented products

- Outstanding guest relations at the theme parks

Ray Kroc, of McDonald's fame, understood his niche in the marketplace. His business plan never included offering nutritious meals or providing a plush physical environment where customers could relax. McDonald's success is based upon:

- Fast, convenient service

- Tasty, reasonably priced meals

- Consistent, predictable customer experience

- Clean environment

To identify what you stand for, ask yourself:

- What are the three or four key results areas in my department for which outstanding performance is required?

- What do I want my department to be known for?

- When I leave this position, what do I want my legacy to be?

Identifying what you stand for is not a theoretical or academic exercise. It helps you determine how you should spend your time and money, what topics you should place on meeting agendas, who you should hire and promote, and what criteria you'll use to reward and hold people accountable.

The Buddha said, "To know and not to do is not to know." This suggests that you demonstrate your commitment to values not through words, but through deeds. Work can be exceedingly fulfilling when your daily activities are in alignment with your values. You don't resent the amount of time and energy you put into your job because you are following your bliss.

On the other hand, you are likely to become extremely frustrated if a plethora of meetings and administrative responsibilities keeps you away from those activities that support your values. If this is the case, meet with your manager to advocate for a better use of your time. Identify which activities you would like to spend a different amount of time on than you do now, and make a case that the proposed change is both desirable and practical.

What Do You Stand For?

Answering the following questions will help you identify what you stand for and establish meaningful priorities for yourself and your department:

- What do you want to have accomplished when you look back on your career? What do you want people to say about you? What will your legacy be?

- Starting today, what must you do to make this vision a reality? What habits would you have to delete from your current leadership style? What is the best use of your time?

- What obstacles (internal or external) stand in the way of your making these changes?

- What steps will you take to overcome these obstacles?

Discussion Questions

Why is it important for people to know what principles you stand for? If asked, could your employees articulate those principles? If they can't, what steps will you take so that everyone is working in support of the same vision?

Are your everyday activities visibly in alignment with your priorities? If not, what are you going to do about it?

---

*Commitment is what transforms a promise into
a reality . . . Commitment is the stuff
that character is made of; the power to change
the face of things. It is the daily triumph
of integrity over skepticism.*

ABRAHAM LINCOLN

5

ESTABLISHING
PERFORMANCE STANDARDS

Meanings are in people, not in words. For example, the term "customer service" means different things to different people. A person might sincerely believe he is providing excellent service while customer feedback indicates that he is rude and indifferent. This is the reason why standards play such a critical role in managing performance.

Well-written standards provide a realistic description of excellent quality, accuracy, quantity, timeliness, thoroughness, and/or cost effectiveness. They describe the way in which the job should be performed, while providing structure and boundaries for appropriate conduct. Performance standards actually increase job satisfaction because employees know when they are successfully performing their jobs. Standards also serve as an objective basis for evaluating employee performance.

Some performance areas, such as attendance or technical competence, are relatively easy to measure. Conduct-related standards such as teamwork or customer service are more difficult to quantify. To measure these behaviors, you need to capture your performance expectations in narrative terms.

The following exercises are designed to help you develop performance standards for teamwork:

Exercise 1. Ask your team members to answer the following questions:

- Regardless of personal feelings toward any member of the team, what should we do to set each other up for success and help each other look good in the eyes of the customer? What behaviors should we avoid?

- What should we do to protect the reputation of our organization? What behaviors should we avoid?

- How can we help make our manager successful and satisfied with her job? What behaviors interfere with her success and job satisfaction?

Exercise 2. Make a list of employees who are positive role models of teamwork. List the specific behaviors they exhibit that contribute to building a cohesive team.

Exercise 3. Convene a meeting of your best team players. Ask them to identify what they consistently do that contributes to building a cohesive department. Also, request that they develop a list of unhelpful teamwork practices that should not be tolerated.

To establish standards for customer service, you will have to drill down in your performance expectations to the job classification level. For example, a nurse and a receptionist on a medical-surgical unit have very different interactions with patients and guests. While there may be much commonality in what is expected and what is not tolerated, your stated performance standards should reflect the differences in their roles.

The following exercise will help you develop performance standards for customer service:

Ask people within each job classification to identify those key interactions with customers in which they have an opportunity to demonstrate outstanding service. These are the moments of truth when there is no second chance to create a positive first impression. Examples include answering the phone, greeting the customer for the first time, having conversations with customers, transferring the customer to another work unit, and concluding the customer interaction.

For each moment of truth:

- Identify what the employee should say or do to make the customer feel welcome, comfortable, secure, heard, understood, informed, and taken seriously. List the desired non-verbal behaviors such as eye contact, facial expression, volume and tone of voice, and posture. Also discuss the employee's responsibility as it relates to professional attire, and issues related to the physical environment such as cleanliness, lighting, seating, and desk appearance.

- List those behaviors that signify indifference or disrespect for the customer. Also, capture non-verbal behaviors that should not be tolerated.

- Identify challenging situations that can arise, such as excessive waiting time before the customer will be served, scheduling conflicts, or dealing with a verbally abusive customer. Describe what the employee should say or do to meet or exceed the customer's expectations. Also, describe actions that may make a bad situation worse.

The purpose of this exercise is to lock in consistency and predictability. After all, service quality should not be contingent upon who is taking care of the customer.

Finalizing and Implementing Standards

Before you lock in your performance standards, ask your team the following questions:

- Are these standards realistic and attainable?

- Is additional training needed to help you meet these standards?

- How can we monitor and evaluate expected behavior?

- Did you have enough input to feel ownership of the standards?

- What should you do if you observe a co-worker not adhering to the performance standards?

Examples of Teamwork and Customer Service Standards

Teamwork

- When finished with your own work, unless it's your break time, offer to help others without being asked. Don't sit in customer lounge areas, read a book, engage in personal phone conversations, gossip, text, or play games on your phone or the computer.

- When you have a disagreement with a co-worker, try to solve the problem at the earliest opportunity by talking directly to the person in private.

- Avoid behaviors that tear down department cohesiveness, such as gossiping, complaining, trash talking, and holding grudges.

Customer Service

- Introduce yourself by name and position when meeting customers for the first time. Smile, maintain eye contact, and give them your undivided attention. If you're not certain how to pronounce their name, ask them. Don't look rushed or disinterested; don't act as if you're doing customers a favor by taking care of them.

- When dealing with an upset customer, confirm your understanding of the complaint; apologize for the inconvenience, delay, or confusion; and partner with the customer to find a solution to the problem.

- Do not get personally defensive. Right or wrong, the customer's perceptions are real and have to be addressed. Never yell, swear, interrupt, or ignore the customer. Get assistance from a co-worker or manager if you're concerned that you may lose your patience and say something you will later regret.

- When a customer makes a request, don't ever say:

  - "It's not my job."

  - "You're not my customer."

  - "I can't help you now because I am going to lunch."

  - "I'm sorry, but we're short staffed today."

Employees' Responsibility to Monitor their Own Behavior

Sometimes an employee will disregard policies and procedures or engage in unprofessional conduct when you're away from the work unit. When this occurs, other employees have an obligation to share their feedback with the person in a direct and respectful manner. There is a natural resistance to doing so, however, because people generally want to avoid potential conflict, or they believe it's not their responsibility to address performance issues. Therefore, teach employees to recognize when it is their responsibility to independently address such issues, how best to handle the conversation, and when to involve you.

It may be helpful to establish ground rules for dialogue. For example, if an employee overhears two co-workers having an argument that could be overheard by customers, she has an obligation to ask them to take their discussion away from the public area. If an employee observes a co-worker having an argument with a customer, he should approach the co-worker by apologizing to the customer for interrupting and then saying to the co-worker, "I need to speak with you right away." When out of earshot of the customer, he should describe to the co-worker what he saw and heard that caused him to be alarmed, and ask if he can help in any way. He should avoid any judgmental comments or accusations, and simply offer help and support. If the co-worker responds defensively, saying something like, "Don't tell me what to do. You're not my manager. Mind your own business," he should reply, "I know I'm not your manager, but I am your co-worker, and we all have a responsibility to help each other do what's in the best interest of the customer."

You may want to consider sharing this dialogue with employees as an example of peer coaching. This will be new for most work teams, but with practice and reinforcement, people will get better at solving problems together without requiring your direct involvement. Once they have a sense of how to give and receive effective feedback to one another in the pursuit of high quality performance, your work unit will be well on its way to creating a culture of accountability.

Setting Standards for Interdepartmental Collaboration

Identify departments with whom you are interdependent, meaning that your team can't accomplish its goals unless that department successfully executes its responsibilities in a timely and effective manner. The other department also has needs and expectations of your team that must be met in order to accomplish its goals.

Meet with representatives of these departments separately to discuss how to communicate effectively and hold each other accountable for a cooperative relationship. Agree to:

- Schedule regular meetings to discuss challenging incidents that were well handled by the two groups. Identify what was done to achieve a positive outcome. Discuss challenging incidents that were not handled well. Was the problem caused by a people or system failure? If you had another chance, what would you do differently to get a better outcome?

- Agree on a protocol for addressing problems and securing closure on issues in a timely fashion. Allowing problems to fester over a sustained period of time erodes trust and invites doubt that a good relationship is possible. The protocol should stipulate that when conflicts arise, managers should not use their employees as a sounding board to criticize members of the other department. Instead, they should attempt to solve the problem by talking directly to one another privately. If necessary, they

can agree to disagree and decide on a third party to
mediate the conflict.

- Conduct periodic team-building workshops to clarify
  roles and responsibilities and to make commitments
  that will help make the other department's job easier,
  more satisfying, and more effective.

Share the results of these discussions with all
the employees of both departments, emphasizing
that seamless customer service can only be achieved
through effective communication with one another.
Develop standards for interdepartmental relations by
using the exercises described for teamwork and customer service on pages 60-61, and solicit everyone's
commitment to meeting performance expectations.

Discussion Questions

What is the risk of developing goals without
accompanying performance standards?

Has your department agreed on what teamwork
and customer service look like for you? Have you identified what behaviors should not be tolerated? If yes,
describe the process you used to develop these performance standards.

*If you don't stand for something,
you'll fall for anything.*

MALCOLM X

INSPECTING WHAT
YOU EXPECT

You don't have the time to micromanage people, hover over them, and watch every move they make. You must find simple, user-friendly strategies to monitor their actual performance against established standards. Listed below are practical monitoring strategies to determine whether people are meeting customer service and teamwork standards.

Monitoring Strategies for Customer Service

- Direct observation: Place yourself in a position to observe first hand your employees' interactions with the customers.

- Review customer satisfaction survey results.

- Interview customers shortly after a service has been rendered to obtain their impressions while still fresh in their minds.

- Document unsolicited customer compliments or complaints.

Monitoring Strategies for Teamwork

- Direct observation: Place yourself in a position to observe employees interacting with one another.

- Document unsolicited compliments or complaints from co-workers within the department.

- Solicit feedback from people in other departments or suppliers who regularly interface with your team.

- Check applicable reports, time sheets, work records, and logs that document productivity.

- Ask people to document their own achievements, mistakes, challenges, and/or status of assigned projects.

- Conduct exit interviews.

Practice "Management by Walking Around"

One of the most effective methods to monitor the way people are interacting with customers and co-workers is to watch them in action. Initially, you may not get an accurate picture of how people usually conduct themselves; your very presence will alter their behavior. Eventually, however, a pattern of practices emerges, and you can more confidently evaluate employees' teamwork and customer service orientation.

Before you schedule times to work alongside and observe your team in action, it is important to communicate the purpose of the activity. Explain that your intent is not to catch them doing something wrong. On the contrary, your observations will provide you with an opportunity to recognize achievement on a timely basis, roll up your own sleeves and offer a helping hand when the need arises, and identify any system barriers to your team's success. It will also provide you with the invaluable opportunity to listen to employee concerns, answer questions, share information, quell rumors, and secure your team's input before making a decision.

In summary, your team can help you develop inspection techniques that are transparent and unobtrusive. You want to avoid creating an intimi-dating or fear-inducing monitoring process in which people feel that their behavior is constantly being scru-tinized. Valid monitoring can only be accomplished if people understand how and why you will be evaluat-ing their performance. This means giving them space to do their work and being as transparent as possible in your monitoring approach.

Provide Employees with Performance Feedback

Once you've developed a practical, user-friendly evaluation system, it's time to talk about how to share the information with your team. The most impactful performance feedback is timely feedback, delivered as soon as possible after an event that is worthy of comment takes place. It is also direct, honest, and unconditionally respectful. Whenever your monitor-ing reveals a need for performance improvement, make certain that you:

- Describe in narrative terms what the person needs to do differently to meet your expectations. Avoid ambiguous and imprecise language or using labels that will put the employee on the defensive. This language is neither instructive nor constructive.

- Do not use the "sandwich" approach to criticism, which recommends that you begin the conversation by recognizing the person for his overall good performance (to soften the blow), next addressing the problematic behavior (the real reason for having the discussion), and ending the meeting with another compliment (to enhance the person's self-esteem). This tactic is both insincere and manipulative. If you make a practice of recognizing people when they do a good job, you won't feel compelled to compliment them when addressing an error in judgment or performance deficiency.

- Avoid yelling or swearing. Don't allow another person's negativity to influence your own conduct. You're not accountable for her behavior, but you are accountable for your reaction to it. If you permit her to provoke you, you're allowing her to control you.

- Be an active listener and respectfully consider the other person's perspective. Avoid interrupting.

- Keep the conversation private. When you criticize someone in front of co-workers or customers, the person has no opportunity to save face and maintain self-esteem. He may plot revenge, and, perhaps more importantly, you will have given the rest of the staff a reason to distrust you.

- Maintain confidentiality. Don't badmouth one employee to another employee, even in private. Chances are good that it will get back to the person. Trust may be irrevocably broken. In addition, other employees will think, "If he talks that way about Bob, I wonder what he says about me behind my back . . ." Always be loyal to those not present.

- Give out sensitive information about employees only to people who have a job-related need to know.

- Remain open and curious rather than jumping to conclusions: Even if you directly observe someone doing something wrong, listen to her perspective before rendering a judgment. Engage her in a dialogue:

  "Help me understand from your perspective what happened."

  "Please explain why you responded as you did."

  "Looking back, what could you have done differently?"

  "What steps will you take to prevent this from reoccurring?"

  "What have you learned from this incident?"

- Avoid apologizing for having this discussion. It detracts from the seriousness of your message.

Providing performance feedback is a necessary and integral part of your job. You can be firm and resolute while treating employees with unconditional respect.

Discussion Questions

Once you have established performance standards, what are the consequences if you don't monitor employee conduct to ensure that it is consistent with your expectations?

Describe how you currently inspect what you expect. What is working well? What could you do differently in order to be more attuned to what is going on in your work unit?

I can accept failure; everyone fails at something.
What I can't accept is not trying.

MICHAEL JORDAN

WHY SOME EMPLOYEES FAIL

There is a variety of reasons why some people fail to meet performance expectations. Listed below are ten of the most common explanations, followed by a discussion of what you can do to address the performance deficiency.

1. Unawareness of Performance Deficits

The person honestly believes that she is doing a good job or that there is nothing wrong with her conduct. While she may understand in a general sense that you are not pleased with her work, she does not know what needs to be done differently to meet your expectations.

Your Responsibility

Establish specific and behaviorally concise performance expectations. Provide frequent feedback to ensure that the person knows how well she is doing in meeting those expectations. Explain what she needs to start doing or stop doing to demonstrate improvement. Include timeframes if indicated. Stipulate the potential consequences for failing to meet expectations.

2. Wrong Person for the Role

The person is simply unable to do the job; he is trying his best, but he does not have the mental and/or physical capacity to achieve the desired results.

Your Responsibility

Don't automatically assume that a person lacks initiative when he does not meet your performance expectations. He may simply be miscast for the role.

Determine if a reasonable accommodation should be made to facilitate the person's success. If appropriate, offer him another position that plays to his strengths. If no internal solution is found, with Human Resources' involvement, offer the person an opportunity to resign in good standing in exchange for career counseling and job search assistance.

3. Insufficient Skill Set

The person has the motivation but lacks the skills to perform the job.

Your Responsibility

Create a training regimen that is tailored to the person's specific need for improvement. Provide "just-in-time training" in which you coach and counsel the person just before she has to deal with a challenging situation; have her perform the task, and shortly thereafter meet with her to assess how she did. Ask her to answer the following questions:

- Are you pleased with the result? If yes, what do you think contributed to your success?"

- If you could change anything, what would you do differently?

The benefit of this approach is that you are proactively setting up the person for success rather than reacting to performance deficiencies. Also, by assessing the quality of performance on an immediate basis, your feedback is likely to be specific and behaviorally concise.

4. Lack of Confidence

The person doubts his ability to do the job. He gets easily discouraged and is his own worst critic.

Your Responsibility

This person may need ample reassurance that he is performing at a competent level. Communicate your sincere confidence in the person's abilities and potential for professional development. Place yourself in a position to catch him doing something right and provide immediate positive feedback.

Don't try to boost the person's self-confidence by lowering your performance standards in order to enable him to succeed. Maintain high performance expectations, provide resources such as coaching and training to facilitate his success, and celebrate achievement, even if improvement comes in increments.

5. Lack of Accountability to the Team

The person's overall demeanor is one of indifference, bordering on contempt toward co-workers. She does just enough to get by and acts like she is doing you a favor when asked to do something that is part of her job.

Your Responsibility

Describe for the person how she is coming across to others based on your own observation and the feedback received from co-workers. If necessary, explain that if enough different people over a sustained period of time say the same negative things about her, they can't all be wrong or be out to get her. Provide a warning that the next time a credible person complains about her, you will investigate the situation, but you can't keep granting her the benefit of the doubt. Corrective action may be administered up to and including discharge.

6. Lack of Respect for Customers

The person shows very little sensitivity to customer needs. The person is cold, abrupt, or argumentative. He always appears to be rushed or too busy to listen to the customer's concerns. You regularly receive unsolicited customer complaints about the employee.

Your Responsibility

Some people lack the empathy and social skills to be employed in the service industry. You can coach the person or have him attend classes on interpersonal relationship skills. Your efforts may be futile, however, if the person has made a habit of practicing thinly disguised contempt toward customers. At some point, you may simply have to document occurrences of impropriety and make a case for discharge, following your organization's corrective action policy.

7. Lack of Role Clarity

The person is dependent on others who are not performing their jobs in a timely and effective manner.

Your Responsibility

Clarify roles and responsibilities so that everyone understands where their job begins, ends, and overlaps with other members of the team. Intervene on the employee's behalf if you believe that her work is being compromised by someone's negligence or incompetence. However, hold her accountable for communicating her needs and expectations to those people who can help or hinder the accomplishment of her goals.

8. Lack of Employee Autonomy

The person believes that he does not have the necessary authority, independence, or autonomy to do his job.

Your Responsibility

If the person has established a record of sound judgment and initiative, he has earned the right to work with autonomy and control over his job. On the other hand, it would be a mistake to grant more discretionary powers to an employee who cuts corners and relaxes policies and procedures when nobody is looking.

Freedom without responsibility is a dangerous thing. Suggest to the person that if he wants to be managed less by you he needs to manage himself more. Stipulate what he needs to do differently to earn your trust and be granted more autonomy and control over his job.

Consider that the problem may be caused by role confusion, which almost always leads to unnecessary conflict. Therefore, take steps to ensure that all employees understand their role in the decision-making process. There are some decisions an employee can make without your prior knowledge or consent. There are other decisions, however, that require your approval before any action is taken. These are decisions that:

- Could have a negative impact on the reputation of the organization or department.

- Have serious budget implications.

- Present legal or ethical implications.

- Could negatively impact team or customer satisfaction.

Meet with individuals to reach a common understanding of each other's role and levels of authority based on various situations that may be encountered.

9. System Failure

The person's performance is adversely affected by ill-conceived organizational processes, procedures, and protocols. For example, there is a lack of materials and supplies, insufficient staffing levels, lack of time to complete tasks, or unrealistic deadlines.

Your Responsibility

Don't hold an employee accountable for a system problem over which she has no control. When a mistake is made, thoroughly investigate the causes of the problem. You may need to clarify or revise a policy or procedure that contributed to the error.

Encourage the person to be on the lookout for system barriers that serve as an impediment to job success. It's everyone's responsibility to look for ways to make the work environment safer, cleaner, friendlier, more efficient, and cost-effective.

Create a retribution-free communication environment in which employees can safely

blow the whistle on unethical or illegal practices. Nothing guarantees that wrongdoing
will continue more than good people who
observe it and feel too unsafe or disempowered
to say or do anything about it.

10. Lack of Motivation Due to Negativity and Cynicism

The person plays the role of victim or
martyr and appears to feel entitled to the job.

Your Responsibility

Despite work frustrations, the employee is
ultimately responsible for her own motivation,
attitude, work ethic, and service orientation.
Communicate that griping and dumping will
not be tolerated. The person must choose to
be a collaborative team player in search of a
solution to the problems she identifies.

She must also understand that her job success and satisfaction are largely influenced
by her own attitude. If it is her habit to evade
responsibility, she may blame the manager or
make excuses such as:

- This is the way I am. I have always been this way.

- I am too old to change now.

- I didn't do it (when she really did).

- I didn't know (when she did or should have).

- I couldn't help it (when she could have).

- I can't do it (when she really doesn't want to try it).

Teach the Benefits of Self-Management

Share with the employee the benefits of holding yourself accountable for your conduct and the effect it has on others. This is an area of professional development that deserves some thoughtful discussion.

Taking responsibility for one's attitude and accepting the consequences of one's actions are preconditions for achieving success and satisfaction at work and in life. Attitude is 10% what happens to you and 90% how you react to it. Two people within a department can experience the same work frustrations. One person says to herself, "I know this job is not perfect, and I certainly don't agree with this decision, but this is a whole lot better than other places I have worked." The other person says, "This decision proves once again that the manager couldn't care less about us," and uses it an excuse to adopt a negative attitude. In short, it's not what happens *to* you that influences your attitude as much as what happens *within* you.

Some people suggest that complaining is cathartic—that it provides an opportunity to blow off steam and reduce tension. Actually, the opposite is true. The very process of complaining helps you to become even more dissatisfied with your life. The Buddhist philosophy has relevance here. It teaches that what you focus on, you get more of. In today's vernacular, this is known as "selective perception." If you ruminate about all of your job frustrations, you may find yourself with no energy left to appreciate the positive aspects of your job.

The social costs may also be high. If you regularly complain about everyday work frustrations and minor inconveniences, nobody will take you seriously when you bring up a problem that really does warrant attention. Therefore, choose your fights with discretion.

You may identify an important problem that can and should be solved, but your communication style is placing people on the defensive. Think about how you can package your ideas in a manner that people are willing to listen to you and how you can listen to people so they feel heard and understood.

Additionally, you will never achieve job satisfaction if you take the good aspects you have for granted. One major source of happiness is gratitude. It is my experience that ungrateful people are never happy. Find an opportunity to ask the person to engage in the following exercises designed to enhance her awareness of the benefits that are derived from working here:

- Make a list of the things you like about your job, work unit, and organization.

- Write down anything that occurred today that brought you a laugh, a feeling of accomplishment, or a closer relationship with a co-worker.

- Talk about a recent challenge you overcame. Describe how it made you feel.

- Thank somebody today for a job well done.

- Commit at least one conscious act of kindness on a daily basis.

As a result of teaching the benefits of accepting accountability for one's conduct and attitude, a person may decide that she simply can't accept and adjust to certain problems; instead of constantly complaining about the situation, it would be better to separate from the job. This may not necessarily be a bad outcome.

Remind the person, however, that while the next organization may not have the same problems that exist where she now is, she will no doubt find a different set of problems to deal with. She will also be bringing her attitude with her wherever she goes.

Explain that there is a graceful way to separate from a job, and that you expect her to:

- Give you ample notice of the resignation.

- Continue to come to work as her current schedule requires, rather than using accumulated short-term disability benefits on the assumption that she is entitled to them, unless she really is sick.

- Do a good job through the last day of employment; don't burn bridges behind you.

Commitments Must be Honored

As long as a person chooses to remain in his current position, the burden is on the employee to inform you of any obstacles that could prevent him from honoring previously established commitments. Sometimes commitments may have to be renegotiated because of changes in the work environment; however, an employee should not be allowed to unilaterally renege on a commitment without consequences. Making excuses after the fact, covering up, and lying by omission are indicators that the person can't be trusted.

While securing employee commitment to produce specific results is ideal, it is not necessary. What is necessary is that the person understands your performance expectations and the consequences for not meeting them.

Try to resolve your differences in a respectful and professional manner. Actively listen to the person and consider his perspective. If no agreement can be reached, document the areas of contention and invite the employee to do the same.

You have the final say, whenever an employee disagrees with a specific performance expectation or refuses to accept an assignment, providing:

- Your expectation is consistent with the organization's mission and values.

- Your expectation is job-related. (It is part of the nature, function, and scope of the job.)

- Your expectation is reasonable and attainable.

- Your expectation does not place the person at risk. What you're asking the person to do is legal, ethical, professional, and safe.

- Your expectation is non-discriminatory. It is based on business necessity and applies to everyone within the same job classification.

- The performance expectation was communicated. The person knew (or was adequately informed) that it was part of the job.

Direct refusal to accept an assignment that meets the criteria above is an act of insubordination. When this occurs, you have three options:

- Consider the person's reason for refusal, and if appropriate, change the assignment based on the person's input.

- Explain why the assignment stands despite the person's objections and that refusal to comply will result in immediate disciplinary action.

- Suggest that the person perform the assignment now and file a grievance later, thereby avoiding formal discipline.

The ball is now in the employee's court to do what is expected or accept the consequences of refusal.

An employee should not commit to achieving a specific result if he is aware of an obstacle to success that is outside his control. When presented with this scenario, you have the following options:

- If the identified obstacle is within your control, remove it, then hold the person accountable for meeting the performance expectation.

- If you can't remove the obstacle, consider revising or eliminating the performance expectation. It would be unfair to hold the person accountable for failing to meet a goal that was unattainable in the first place.

- Maintain the performance expectation if you believe that (despite the obstacle) the goal can be accomplished.

To determine if your performance expectations are reasonable, ask yourself the following questions:

- Are other employees able to achieve the desired results given the same limited resources? If yes, why is this person an outlier?

- Is there enough time to accomplish the desired result?

- Are staffing levels adequate?

- Is the budget sufficient?

- Has training or coaching been made available?

- Have sufficient materials, supplies, and equipment been provided?

- Am I accessible and responsive to the person's concerns?

Problems versus Realties

Maintain your high standards, but be aware of the conditions on the ground that impact achievement. There is no problem so difficult that it can't be solved. If it can't be solved, it's not a problem; it's a reality. Employees need to learn to recognize the difference so that they can accept and adjust to realities and solve the problems that are within their control.

One source of employee dissatisfaction is the perception that you are not doing what is necessary to support them in their work. You may have a real conflict on your hands if your team thinks an obstacle to success or satisfaction is a problem that can be solved when you know that it is outside your direct control or sphere of influence to overcome. If this condition persists for a sustained period of time, your team will see you as being insensitive to their needs. After all, if you cared about them, you would have corrected the problem by now.

Consider the following exercise to ensure that employees have realistic expectations of what can and can't be changed:

Step One

Discuss with your team the difference between problems and realities. A problem is an obstacle to job success and satisfaction that can be solved within our department. We are not dependent on another work unit or higher ups to fix this. We own it. A reality is an obstacle to job success and satisfaction that is outside our direct control.

Step Two

Have your team brainstorm all of their perceived obstacles to job success and satisfaction. This list includes everything they complain about over the water cooler, during coffee breaks, or with their friends and families.

Step Three

Take each item on the list and determine whether it is a problem or a reality. Examples of realities include budgetary constraints, space limitations, and organizational restructuring resulting in staff reductions. Another example may be that if you're in the service industry, you will always have some customers who are demanding or harsh. How the customer behaves is outside of your control; however, how you respond to the customer is within your control.

If people perceive an item on the list to be a problem and you know it to be a reality, patiently explain your prior attempts to improve the situation and why your efforts proved to be in vain. You may personally identify with your employees' frustrations and agree with their assessment of the need for positive change, but don't blame higher-ups or peers for the situation.

Employees will benefit from your sharing the big picture and placing the situation in the proper context. For example, you may say, "I know the current situation does not meet our department's specific needs, but let me share with you the rationale for the action taken."

Step Four

After you have distinguished problems from realities, select the top three problems that, if solved, would best meet the following criteria:

- The payoff for solving the problem is great.

- The degree of effort is reasonable.

- The probability of success is high.

Step Five

Identify the best course of action for each of the three selected problems. Develop methods and timetables for implementation. Assign roles and responsibilities, and determine how you will monitor and evaluate outcomes.

Don't engage in this process unless you are confident that there will be sufficient follow-through to solve the problems you choose to work on. People will get cynical if you don't solve problems that are completely within your control.

Step Six

Discuss how the team can best accept and adjust to realities. Address the futility of complaining about things we can't do anything about.

Engaging the team in an exercise such as this one creates a sense of ownership of the work environment. Empowering the team to solve its own problems will serve to strengthen the foundation of your culture of accountability.

Holding People Accountable for Continuous Learning

Regardless of an employee's age or tenure, don't allow anyone to rest on his laurels. Develop a learning culture within your department in which everyone's skills are expected to be state-of-the-art in their respective fields.

- Conduct a needs assessment to identify training and development opportunities.

- Establish individual and team learning goals and integrate them into the performance appraisal process.

- Conduct continuing education workshops on paid, productive work time. Offer the sessions at various times to facilitate attendance. Do not hesitate to make the program mandatory. Often the people who need the workshop the most are the ones most likely to find excuses for not attending. Provide an accountability loop that requires employees to share with you what they learned and how they will apply the information.

- Encourage people to become active members of their professional associations, attend programs, and bring back what they learned for the benefit of the team.

- Create a first-rate new employee orientation system that ensures that new hires have the necessary skills to perform their jobs. Also attend to new employees' psychosocial needs, such as celebrating their arrival, making proper introductions, and accompanying them for meals. Establish a zero tolerance policy for anyone who attempts to make the work environment inhospitable, intimidating, or in any way unwelcoming for new hires.

- Demonstrate that you value innovation. Encourage people to look for ways to make their work easier, more efficient, faster, cleaner, friendlier, and more cost-effective.

Discussion Questions

Have you ever had an employee who was technically competent but whose behavior wreaked havoc on group morale? How did you handle the situation?

Have you ever had an employee who directly refused to comply with one of your directives? How did you handle the situation?

One measure of leadership is the caliber
of people who choose to follow you.

DENNIS A. PEER

8

MANAGING DISRUPTIVE BEHAVIOR

You have a legal obligation to maintain a hostility-free work environment and should not tolerate any form of abusive, degrading, or humiliating behavior. Conduct that is grounds for immediate disciplinary action on the first offense includes:

- Verbal abuse, including swearing, name-calling, personal insults, and threatening remarks.

- Any actions that have the potential to harm or endanger others.

- Non-verbal abuse, including violating someone's personal space, yelling, stomping feet, pounding the table, throwing objects, clenching fists, or any form of aggressive physical conduct such as poking, pushing, or punching.

- Behaviors that cause workplace distress, including practical jokes at the expense of others, pranks, gossiping, or perpetrating rumors that impugn reputation.

- Behavior that mocks mental or physical vulnerability.

- Discrimination or harassment based on race, color, religion, gender, ethnic or national origin, age, sexual orientation, marital status, or disability.

- Sexual harassment, including offensive remarks about looks, clothing, or body parts; touching that makes someone feel uncomfortable such as patting, pinching, intentionally brushing against another's body; sexual or lewd jokes; and sexually suggestive gestures, letters, texts, or emails.

- Insubordination, including direct refusal to comply with a manager's directive, aggressive conduct or threatening remarks directed toward the manager.

- Any statements or conduct that compromise the reputation of the organization.

Your response to such aberrant behavior must be calm, quick, and decisive. This type of conduct is a testing of boundaries or limits. If you are reluctant to uphold standards of behavior, others will begin to test how far they can go before you push back. What you accept is what you teach.

A Seven-Step Model for Managing Dysfunctional Conduct

1. Don't wait too long to address attitudinal and behavioral issues. One person's negativity can be very contagious. Even if the person identifies a real problem that needs to be solved, you still must hold the person accountable for counter-productive responses to the issue.

2. Describe in specific terms the negative behavior and its impact on teamwork or customer service.

3. Identify alternative constructive behaviors that the person is expected to demonstrate.

4. State the consequences for noncompliance.

5. Offer resources within the organization that could help the person succeed in altering his response to work frustrations.

6. Monitor and evaluate the person's progress. Place yourself in a position to observe the person's conduct or solicit feedback from others.

7. Recognize improvement or mete out consequences for failure to correct her behavior.

The Importance of Documentation

From a Human Resources perspective, if an incident of wrongdoing is not documented, it never happened. Without sufficient documentation, you place yourself at risk if an employee challenges a performance appraisal or disciplinary action, claiming it is unfair or unwarranted.

It is critical that you adhere to your own organization's policies and procedures for corrective action. As a general rule, however, use the performance appraisal process to document performance deficiencies and the disciplinary action process for documenting attendance issues, disruptive conduct, acts of insubordination, or the violation of policies and procedures.

The first step in most progressive disciplinary action policies is a coaching session or verbal warning. Document the coaching/warning session by creating an anecdotal record of the conversation which is kept in a secure area of your office or home. Anecdotal records help you document a pattern of employee conduct. They also serve as evidence that you have tried to correct the problem before beginning the formal disciplinary action process. You may choose to provide a copy of the anecdotal record to the person and ask him to sign it, but you are not legally bound to do so.

The next steps in most corrective action processes are a written warning followed by suspension and discharge. Employees have a right to review and challenge your documentation. You stand a good chance of overcoming an employee grievance if your documentation includes the following elements:

- The date and time of the occurrence.

- A description of the event that captures all of the important facts, including testimony from offended parties and witnesses to the event.

- The negative impact of the offense (or potential impact if caught in time).

- The policy, procedure, or departmental protocol that was violated, and in what ways the person's conduct is inconsistent with the organization's mission, vision, and values.

- Any documentation of previous incidents that demonstrate a pattern of conduct (if applicable).

- The person's response to the allegations: Does he admit or deny wrongdoing? Does he acknowledge the seriousness of the mistake or does he minimize it? Does he accept the corrective action as legitimate, or does he believe it is unwarranted and unfair? If indicated, capture the person's defensive response when you confronted him about the occurrence (closed posture, lack of eye contact, interrupting, raised voice, swearing, etc.).

If the person indicates that he believes that the corrective action is unfair, include his version of events and attach it to the record. Recommend that he contact Human Resources to appeal your decision. This will convey a message that you are confident that any independent investigation would support the action taken.

Get Your Manager's and the Human Resources Department's Support

From the very beginning of the corrective action process, establish an ongoing dialogue with your own manager and your Human Resources (HR) representative regarding the nature and scope of the problem. State that it is your intention to follow HR policies and procedures, and ask what is required to secure their support.

It is the role of HR to ensure consistent management practices within and between departments. HR also needs to be confident that all disciplinary actions can be successfully defended if challenged by someone outside the organization. Therefore, be prepared to answer the following questions:

- Is the corrective action consistent with how you have handled similar infractions in the past? Can you provide examples to show that you're not treating this person any differently from others?

- If this is the person's first offense, explain why it warrants formal disciplinary action as opposed to beginning with a verbal warning.

- Did you thoroughly investigate the situation, and are you confident that your conclusions will hold up under scrutiny?

- If an objective person were to look at your documentation, would she conclude that your corrective action is reasonable?

Discharging an Employee

Good intentions matter and effort is always appreciated. However, it's your job to create and nurture a team that is capable of achieving desired outcomes. Despite your best efforts to facilitate performance improvement, you may on occasion have to terminate an employee. Don't burden yourself with guilt. You provided the employee every opportunity to succeed if:

- You communicated the performance standards by which the person will be evaluated.

- Your performance expectations were job-related, reasonable, and attainable.

- The person was provided the policies, procedures, and protocols for performing the job.

- You provided resources such as coaching and training to set the person up for success.

- You ensured that there were no system barriers that served as an impediment to success.

- The person received timely performance feedback.

- The person was warned of the consequences for failing to meet performance expectations.

You did everything within reason to help the employee meet your performance expectations. Despite your best efforts, he lacked the skill or motivation to succeed. Control over the employee's performance is an illusion. You can only control the consequences of his actions. You don't really "manage" employees; they manage themselves. You manage their performance.

Discussion Questions

Do more employees get discharged because they lack the will to succeed at meeting performance expectations or because they lack the skill to do the job? Explain your answer.

Why would adequate documentation be important to a Human Resources manager's decision to support or fail to support a manager's corrective action?

In matters of style, swim with the current; in matters of principle, stand like a rock.

THOMAS JEFFERSON

MAKING PERFORMANCE
APPRAISALS RELEVANT

A high percentage of both managers and employees look forward to the performance appraisal interview as much as they do a visit to the dentist for a root canal. Done properly, however, you can leverage the annual appraisal to enhance performance and improve the manager-employee relationship. At its best, it can provide an opportunity for growth and development for both parties.

There is no one correct method to conduct a performance appraisal interview, but there are specific steps you can take to achieve a meaningful dialogue.

These steps are presented in sequential order for your consideration.

Step One: Prepare for the Performance Appraisal Interview

- A week or two before the scheduled performance appraisal interview, ask the employee to complete a self-evaluation form to be shared with you either before or during the meeting. The self-evaluation form should include:

  - A review of the job description to ensure its accuracy.

  - A summary of the person's strengths, contributions, and accomplishments.

  - Opportunities for performance improvement.

  - Obstacles to success.

  - Goals for the coming year.

  - Expectations of the manager in order to facilitate the employee's job success.

- Read past appraisals to review past accomplishments or performance deficiencies that were singled out for improvement.

- Prepare an initial draft appraisal, stating that you are open to making changes based on the person's input during the meeting. Your draft should address the same issues as the person's self-appraisal: strengths and contributions, opportunities for improvement, goals for the coming year, and what you can do to help the person succeed.

- Privacy is critical. Select a meeting place where no one can overhear the discussion. If you don't have an office, reserve a conference room, borrow an office, or find some other private area.

- Allow sufficient time to conduct the interview, especially if you will be addressing sensitive performance issues.

- Make necessary arrangements so that you will not be interrupted during the meeting.

- Create a seating arrangement that makes the employee as comfortable as possible and that is conducive to dialog.

Step Two: Conduct the Performance Appraisal Interview

- Begin by asking the person to share her self-appraisal, beginning with the strengths and contributions she brings to the table. Compare this list with your own assessment of the person's strengths and acknowledge agreement as indicated. Don't get into an argument if you disagree with any item on the person's strength and contribution list. Simply ask the person to support her assessment and indicate your intent to address this issue later on in the discussion.

- Next, ask the person to share how she can improve her performance and compare this list with your own assessment. You can either agree with the person's assessment of her need for improvement, indicate that you think she is doing better than her assessment indicates, or share additional needs for positive change that were not on her list.

- Establish a goal for each need for improvement. To ensure that your expectations for positive change are clear, state what she needs to start or stop doing to demonstrate improvement.

- Consider adding a learning objective to ensure that the person remains current in her knowledge and skill sets. Regardless of age or tenure, the person should not be allowed to rest on her laurels. Stagnation sets in when a person stops learning.

- Secure a commitment from the person that confirms she has the will, skills, and resources necessary to meet the performance expectations.

- Solicit feedback on your own performance. For example, ask the person what you can do to facilitate her job success and satisfaction. Based on the feedback, consider making your own commitment for positive change.

Step Three: Complete the Performance Appraisal

- After the interview, review your notes on what was discussed. Focus on areas of agreement and points where you still may differ. If appropriate, make changes on the final performance appraisal based on feedback you received during the discussion.

- Provide a final copy to the employee. If necessary, invite him to put in writing specific issues of contention, attach it to the record, and send a final copy to Human Resources.

It is desirable but not necessary for the person to embrace the need for performance improvement. It is imperative, however, that the person understands your specific expectations for change and the consequences for not meeting these expectations.

If indicated, schedule another meeting within a couple of weeks of the appraisal to create an action plan, including methods, timetables, evaluation criteria, and monitoring strategies.

Don't wait a full year to conduct the next performance appraisal if you have identified significant performance deficiencies. Schedule a series of interim evaluations (perhaps every 90 days) to ensure that the person knows where she stands relative to your expectations.

In most organizations, a person can be involuntarily discharged based on a series of interim appraisals that indicate a failure to meet performance standards. For example, after the third consecutive 90-day appraisal that documents the person's performance deficiencies, the manager can put in writing: "Failure to meet these expectations within the next three months may result in termination of employment."

A Performance Appraisal Template

While each organization has its own performance appraisal templates, this form contains the basic points that need to be addressed. Consider using it as you prepare for your discussion with each employee.

Employee's strengths, contributions, and accomplishments:

- Employee's opportunities for performance improvement: For each item, describe what the employee must start or stop doing in order to meet your performance expectations.

- How you will you monitor and evaluate performance improvement:

- Obstacles that may hinder the employee's success at meeting expectations:

- What you can do to facilitate the employee's performance improvement:

Common Mistakes Made During Performance Appraisals

Listed below are common mistakes made during the performance appraisal interview. Think about the negative effect each of these mistakes has on the employee.

- The manager fails to complete the appraisal on time or skips the process all together.

- The manager puts very little visible effort into the appraisal. He completes the checklist but provides no documentation to support his conclusions.

- The manager simply hands the completed evaluation form to the employee, requests that it be read in silence, asks if the person has any questions, and requests the person's signature. An equally inappropriate variation of this approach is for the manager to read the evaluation out loud, ask if there are any questions, and request the person's signature.

- The manager allows recent events, either positive or negative, to affect the overall evaluation. The appraisal is not an accurate reflection of the person's overall quality of performance.

- The manager allows a personal relationship with the person (positive or negative) to affect the appraisal.

- The manager does not level with the person regarding the need for improvement. The person leaves the meeting thinking that her quality of work is acceptable.

- The manager's comments are general and ambiguous. If feedback is not specific and behaviorally concise, the person does not know what he needs to do differently to meet the manager's expectations.

- The primary focus of the meeting is on past performance without paying enough attention to setting goals for the coming evaluation period.

- The manager and employee can't reach an agreement. The appraisal interview turns into an argument with both sides trying to change the other's opinion. The appraisal process becomes deadlocked. Both parties leave the meeting feeling frustrated.

Discussion Questions

What message do you convey to employees when you skip, delay, or put little visible effort into their performance appraisals?

Do you agree that there should be no surprises or new issues raised on an employee's performance appraisal? Explain your answer.

EPILOGUE

There is only one good reason for wanting to be manager: It places you in a pivotal position to make a positive difference on behalf of the organization, employees, and the customers you serve. You can inspire people to realize their full potential by expecting them to do their very best, being there for them when they need you, encouraging them, and celebrating their achievements.

Positional power gives you the right to tell employees what to do, but your personal credibility is required to secure their full commitment. What follows is a summary of best performance management practices that will put you in a position to maximize your personal credibility:

- Be grounded in values. Identify and communicate what you stand for.

- Establish high performance standards that support your values and that secure employee commitment to meet or exceed expectations.

- Lead by example. Model the attitude and behavior expected of employees.

- Hire people who are self-motivated, with a strong work ethic and desire to serve. The people you employ are a reflection of your values.

- Ensure that people understand the results to be achieved and the role they play to achieve positive outcomes. Provide them the appropriate amount of freedom, autonomy, and control over their jobs.

- Remove any system barriers to success that are within your control.

- Train and develop people to set them up for success. Create a learning culture.

- Monitor and evaluate performance.

- Recognize achievement.

- Teach all employees how to hold themselves accountable for positive outcomes.

Management can be very rewarding when you use your position to serve, not control. And, if you do it right, when you leave your position, you can say with justifiable pride, that you made a positive difference.

Good luck in your journey!

GLOSSARY OF KEY TERMS

Accountability: Ownership for the consequences of one's decisions and actions.

Commitment: The act of binding oneself, intellectually and psychologically, to a course of action. It implies an allegiance to a goal and a determination to deliver on agreed upon results.

Culture: The set of attitudes, values, and practices that characterizes a work group; a way of thinking or acting that is not necessarily captured in official policy and procedural manuals.

Influence: The capacity to affect the opinions or actions of others through the art of persuasion and the establishment of personal credibility. Influential people are perceived to be trustworthy, believable, admirable, and transparent.

Leadership: The art of communicating a clear and compelling vision and securing voluntary

THE POWER OF SHARED VISION

collaborators who commit to achieving goals that transcend individual self-interests. Leadership includes modelling behaviors expected of others and creating a positive work environment that is conducive to employee job success and satisfaction.

Management: The practice of identifying what needs to be done, establishing roles and responsibilities, and determining methods and timetables for accomplishment. Activities associated with management include goal setting, planning, organizing, delegating, developing performance standards, and monitoring and evaluating outcomes.

Organizational Politics: The use of power and social networking to achieve changes that benefit the organization or individual. People who use politics to their advantage place themselves in a strategic position to shape and influence decisions and build alliances with individuals who can help them accomplish their goals.

Positional Power: The official authority derived from rank or office to require or prohibit specific actions, make changes with or without securing employee input, assign work, evaluate performance, and mete out consequences for non-compliance.

Problems versus Realities: Within the context of a professional environment, a problem is an obstacle to employee job success and satisfaction that is within the manager's control or sphere of influence to solve. A reality is an obstacle that the manager can't do anything about. People need to actively work toward solving problems and to accept and adjust to realities.

Shared Vision: An aspirational description of what a work group can accomplish when people are committed to achieving a common goal (Senge, 1990, pp. 192-211).[1]

---

1. Senge, P. (1990). *The fifth discipline: The art and practice of the learning organization*. New York, NY: Doubleday/Currency.

ABOUT MICHAEL HENRY COHEN

Mike Cohen is a nationally recognized workshop leader and consultant specializing in leadership and team development, organizational communications, employee relations, conflict management and customer service. He has taught Interpersonal Communications, Group Process and Organizational Behavior at Northwestern, Roosevelt, and Dominican Universities, and conducts leadership effectiveness programs for organizations throughout the United States.

Mike served as Director of Employee Relations and Development and Vice President of Human Resources at Weiss Memorial Hospital, Chicago, for 12 years. He holds a Master of Arts degree in Communication Studies from Northwestern University. He is the author of numerous articles and four previous books, *On-the-Job Survival Guide, What You Accept is What You Teach, The Power of Self Management,* and *Time to Lead.*

Information on Michael H. Cohen's management
and employee development workshops can be
obtained by perusing his web page,
www.michaelhcohenconsulting.com,
or by writing to:

Michael H. Cohen
333 N. Euclid Avenue • Oak Park, IL 60302
708.386.1968 • canoepress@yahoo.com

Books by MICHAEL H. COHEN

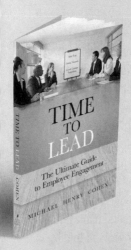

A back-to-basics approach to employee engagement, *Time to Lead* provides common sense leadership practices for busy leaders like you. It is a practical resource on how to address your administrative responsibilities while increasing your presence with employees and customers. Each goal focused exercise and self-assessment tool comes directly from the collective experiences of leaders like you. Softcover, 240 pages. (2011)

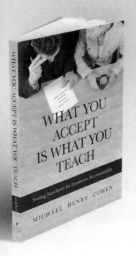

This book provides practical advice to managers on how to hold employees accountable for a strong work ethic, intrinsic motivation, a positive attitude and constructive conduct toward customers and co-workers. It describes a leader's rights and responsibilities relative to maintaining standards for teamwork and customer service. It discusses how to effectively confront and set limits with employees who demonstrate counter productive and passive-aggressive behaviors that raise havoc on group morale. Over 35,000 copies sold. Softcover, 183 pages. (2007)

Books by MICHAEL H. COHEN

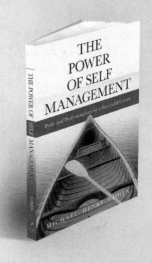

This practical employee companion to *What You Accept is What You Teach* helps staff prepare themselves for the constantly changing health care environment. Learn how to be an outstanding "Organizational Citizen" by developing effective problem solving and "Change-Agent" skills. Develop conflict resolution competence and assertive "Fair-Fighting" skills to deal with difficult co-workers, managers and physicians. Empower yourself to take complete responsibility for your own job success, satisfaction, intrinsic motivation, work and service ethic—regardless of the environment you work in. Softcover, 159 pages. (2008)

ORDER FORM

1. Call toll-free 800.728.7766 x4 and use your Visa, Mastercard, Discover, American Express or a company purchase order

2. Order Online at: www.chcm.com, click on Store.

3. Mail your order with pre-payment or company purchase order to:

   Creative Health Care Management
   5610 Rowland Road, Suite 100
   Minneapolis, MN 55343
   Attn: Resources Department

4. Fax your order to: 952.854.1866

CREATIVE

HEALTH CARE

MANAGEMENT

Product	Price	Quantity	Subtotal	TOTAL
B660: *The Power of Shared Vision*	$14.00			
B605: *Time to Lead*	$19.95			
B519: *The Power of Self Management*	$15.00			
B558: *What You Accept is What You Teach*	$16.00			
Please call 800.728.7766 x4 for a shipping estimate.				
Order TOTAL				

Need more than one copy? We have quantity discounts available.

Quantity Discounts (Books Only)		
10–49 = 10% off	50–99 = 20% off	100 or more = 30% off

Payment Methods: ☐ Credit Card ☐ Check ☐ Purchase Order PO# _____

Credit Card	Number	Expiration	AVS (3 digits)
Visa / Mastercard / Discover / AMEX	– – –	/	
Cardholder address (if different from below):	Signature:		

Customer Information	
Name:	
Title:	
Company:	
Address:	
City, State, Zip:	
Daytime Phone:	
Email:	

Satisfaction guarantee: If you are not satisfied with your purchase, simply return the products within 30 days for a full refund.
For a free catalog of all our products, visit www.chcm.com or call 800.728.7766 x4.